Teach Your Child To Swim Through Games And Play

From Tots to Teens

60 games that use the power of play to embed basic swimming skills and make your child a happy and confident swimmer

Mark Young

Teach Your Child To Swim Through Games And Play

A Catalogue record for this book is available from the British Library
ISBN 978-0-9954842-8-3

Published by: Educate & Learn Publishing, Hertfordshire, UK

Illustrations and diagrams by Mark Young, courtesy of Poser V6.0

Design and typeset by Mark Young

Front cover images courtesy of Shutterstock.com

Note: This book is intended for guidance and support only. It is recommended that the material contained here should accompany swimming lessons conducted by a qualified swimming instructor. Neither the author nor the publisher can accept responsibility for any injury or loss sustained as a result of the use of this material.

Author Online!

For more resources and swimming help visit Mark Young's website at

www.swim-teach.com

Mark Young is a well-established swimming instructor with decades of experience teaching thousands of adults and children to swim. He has taken scared children and adults who fear water and made them happy and confident swimmers. He has also turned many of average ability into advanced swimmers. This book draws on his experiences as both a swimming teacher and a parent to bring together this informative and detailed guide to teaching your child how to swim.

Also by Mark Young

Teaching Guides
101 Swimming Lesson Plans For Swimming Teachers
How To Be A Swimming Teacher
How To Teach Front Crawl
How To Teach Breaststroke
How To Teach Backstroke
How To Teach Butterfly

Learn to Swim Guides
The Complete Beginners Guide to Swimming
How To Swim Front Crawl
How To Swim Breaststroke
How To Swim Backstroke
How To Swim Butterfly
The Swimming Strokes Book

**An electronic version of this book is available from
www.swim-teach.com**

Contents   Page

'In every job that must be done, there is an element of fun.
You find the fun, and - SNAP - the job's a game'

Mary Poppins

Introduction

'I'm Mark Young, a swimming teacher with 30 years experience, and let me tell you, teaching my own three children to swim was a nightmare!

Each time we went to the swimming pool, I'd automatically go into 'swimming teacher' mode and attempt to teach them the conventional  *way, the same way that I'd successfully taught hundreds of children before them. But they just did not listen. Why would they? 'We're in the pool with Dad. We don't have to listen to him. We're here to have fun', they would think. They just wanted to play. So, I gave up trying to teach them and let them play.*

That's when it hit me. By playing and doing their own thing, they were discovering the water for themselves. When I joined in with their play, they naturally engaged with me, as any child would with their parent. So I then began to weave in some basic swimming skills and elements of swimming lessons into their games and, because it was a game, they were willing participants. Without knowing, they were learning how to swim as part of their play.

I now have three very happy and confident swimmers who didn't really need a teacher. They just wanted someone to play with.'

'Play is the foundation of learning, creativity, self-expression, and constructive problem-solving. It's how children wrestle with life to make it meaningful.'

Susan Linn, psychologist and writer

Safety first!

Health And Safety

Taking children swimming

Children can benefit enormously from learning to swim and being confident in and around water; however, as parents and carers, there are some essential safety measures to consider.

If you are taking a young child swimming, find out whether your local pool offers 'parent and toddler' sessions. Pools that offer toddlers a separate swimming area or shallow paddling pool are also worth considering. Building up your child's water confidence is probably easier if no older children splash around them and jump in and out.

Consider the timing of your visit. If your child is very young, you may want to try and choose a time when the pool is quieter. Generally, do not take children swimming after a main meal; wait at least an hour before allowing them to swim.

What age to start swimming?

Many swimming associations advise taking a baby swimming to an adequately heated and maintained public pool from the age of six months.

It is important to take your baby swimming and expose them to water from an early age. Contact with water encourages the desire to swim and reduces the chances of a child developing a fear of water. However, it is essential to remember that a baby is vulnerable for several reasons:

- Babies lose heat more quickly than adults, so the pool temperature should not be too cold, and your baby should not remain in the pool too long.
- Swimming pools use chemicals to sterilise the water, a baby's skin is more delicate than adults and the chemicals may have an adverse effect.
- Although the chlorine or ozone used in pools makes transmitting infections unlikely, waiting until your baby has completed the standard course of vaccine injections is a good idea.

Hygiene

Practising good hygiene when taking a baby or young child swimming is paramount. A swim nappy is essential to prevent faecal water contamination. If this does happen by accident or the baby vomits, contact a staff member immediately.

Other hygiene measures to consider:

- Do not take a baby swimming if they have a tummy upset or suffer from a cold or virus.
- Ensure that children shower before entering the pool to remove sweat and dirt.

- Children with long hair should have it tied up and preferably wear a swimming cap.
- Parents should remove any jewellery.
- Do not allow the children to chew gum or eat whilst they are in the pool area.

Supervision

Constant supervision of children whilst at the swimming pool is essential. Although drownings in pools are extremely rare, accidents happen, so children are at risk, and toddlers are the most vulnerable. It is insufficient to rely solely on the lifeguard's supervision at the poolside.

When you enter the pool for the first time, locate the deep and shallow end, any sudden changes in depth and where the lifeguards are stationed, in case you need their assistance. Be particularly vigilant in 'leisure pools' where there may be several features within the pool, like flumes, fountains and waves.

If swimming with more than one child, never leave one child in the pool whilst taking the other into the changing rooms. Your child is a non-swimmer, so they will need you to assist them in the swimming pool. Younger children who are out of their depth in all, or most of, the pool will need physical support. Because supervision does need to be constant, understand that you will not have the opportunity to swim and exercise yourself.

How To Use This Book

13

The games and how they work

The games and activities in this book are all based on the basic building blocks of learning how to swim. Each game focuses on a particular aspect or combination of parts of swimming, so while your child is busy playing, they are learning a specific skill.

The essential skills the children focus on include:

- Getting used to the water
- Moving around the pool
- Breathing
- Floating
- Submerging
- Gliding
- Kicking their legs
- Pulling with their arms

Each game or activity shows what skill your child is learning and outlines the aim of the game from a learning-to-swim point of view.

Each game has a difficulty rating, from 1 to 3 stars, where 1 star is easy, 2 medium and 3 is hard. It also outlines any equipment you need, key phrases your child needs to hear, and how the game can progress if your child becomes confident or finds it easy.

Each game is set out in the following way:

Sail The Raft the name of the game
Skill: the swimming skill or skills being taught
Aim: what the game is aiming to achieve
Difficulty: ★ difficulty level ★=easy ★ ★=medium ★ ★ ★=hard
Equipment: equipment needed for this game

How to set up and play the game
This activity is performed in water that your child can stand in. Your child holds a float or kickboard...

Key phrases: Phrases to say to your child to help encourage and focus on relevant parts of their body.

Progression: Possible ways to make the game more challenging if your child finds it easy.

Progression or regression?

Each game or activity has a suggested progression designed to move your child on and ensure they make progress. It's up to you as their parent or carer to use your instincts and judgment to decide this. If your child becomes confident and finds a game easy, it's probably time to make it more challenging.

The progressions for each game are only suggestions. There are a few quick ways to make *any* game more challenging. These include:

- Add a breathing technique, such as blowing bubbles, to the game.
- Submerging partially or entirely under the water.
- Slowing the game down, particularly if it involves breathing or submerging. Slowing down will help your child control their breath.
- Playing the game in deeper water, depending on the type of game.
- Reducing or removing buoyancy aids.

When to remove buoyancy aids?

Reducing or removing buoyancy aids from your child is necessary if they are to make progress and learn to swim. However, suggesting this to your child can cause some anxiety and present a challenge, as many children become dependent on them. Their buoyancy aids can become their security, so they are often reluctant to go without them.

Reassurance is vital here, especially if your child is anxious. As their parent or carer, you will become their physical support. Standing to their side and holding them lightly around the waist or facing them with a single hand supporting their belly are two methods of reassuring and assisting their buoyancy.

As they get used to your assistance, you can loosen your grip and gradually reduce the amount of physical support you provide. Your child may instinctively try to grip you as you loosen your grip, and this will almost certainly be the case with anxious children. Try relaxing your grip for a second or two before reapplying, so they know you are still there and have not let them go completely.

During this process of reducing your physical support, you will get a feel for their level of buoyancy and how well they can keep themselves afloat. If you feel your child cannot keep themselves afloat or they are too anxious, keep the support in place and be patient. It may take several weeks for them to become confident and strong. Positive verbal reassurance is vital at all times during this process. Phrases like *'you are doing great', 'don't worry, I've got you'* and *'keep going, I'm here'* will help keep them calm and reassured.

'Children learn through doing – play is how they explore their world, learn how to assess risk, try things out and get to know themselves.'

Bethe Almeras, author and educational speaker

Equipment

Equipment

The games in this book use the minimum amount of equipment, and they are low cost, easy to use, pack, and store. The toys and floats needed to carry out the activities and play the games are affordable and easy to take to and from the swimming pool.

Many games do not need any equipment, and those that do, require the very basics. You will need the following:

- Floats or kickboards
- Pool noodle (sometimes called a woggle)
- Small toys that float
- Toys that sink
- ball

All of the equipment listed above are available online and are very affordable.

Floats and kickboards

When used correctly, swimming floats can help develop specific parts of your child's technique. They are suitable for non-swimmers up to advanced swimmers and can be used by adults and children.

Swimming teachers use swim floats as part of lessons for many different exercises. Non-swimmers can use them to strengthen, and established swimmers to isolate and perfect technique.

For example, the weak non-swimmer can use two floats, one placed under each arm, to help strengthen their leg kick. The floats will provide stability and help boost confidence whilst encouraging a fast and furious leg kick.

 Floats are very versatile, and children can use them in various games and activities. They can double as ships, cargo carriers and speed boats as they distract your child from the chore of learning.

You must note, however, that a child using a float without any other buoyancy aids requires close supervision.

Common mistakes to watch out for

Using a float incorrectly is difficult because they are such a simple piece of swimming equipment. However, there are a couple of points to watch out for when using floats to teach your child.

Firstly, it is common for children to grip the float too tightly, especially if they are nervous beginners. They squeeze the float in their hand, resulting in a very tired hand grip and the focus away from the part of their swimming they are supposed to concentrate on.

Secondly, it is common for children to bare their weight onto the float, causing it to submerge. Once again, this is easily done by the nervous beginner as they attempt to climb above the water surface instead of lying on the surface. Reassuring them and helping them to relax by advising them to *'let the float support you'*, will go some way to helping your child to get the most out of using the floats.

Woggle or Noodle

One of the most popular buoyancy aids, the swimming noodle, is a

simple polythene foam cylinder widely used during swimming lessons. Sometimes called a 'woggle', it is cheap to make, buy, and very easy to use.

The main advantage is that it provides a high level of support while allowing your child to move their arms and legs. They can move around independently and experience propulsion through the water from both the arms and the legs.

The noodle is very versatile, and as it is not a fixed aid, it can be used and removed easily. It can also add a sense of fun to swimming as it can be tucked under the arms on the front and the back as well as placed between the legs and used as a 'seahorse'.

Whilst the noodle allows freedom of movement, watch out for your nervous child clamping it between their body and arms, as this will restrict their movement.

Sinkers

Sinkers are objects such as sticks, hoops and toys that sink to the bottom of the pool. They are a great way to teach your child breath control by encouraging them to submerge.

Sinkers can be used in both shallow and deep water and vary in design to cater for a range of ages.

To children, sinkers are the equivalent of toys, and a parent with a creative imagination can use them to spark excitement and get fantastic results.

Floating Toys

Floating toys come in all shapes and sizes and are usually water themed. They are bright and fun, which makes them appealing to small children. Most importantly, they are small enough to be picked up and held in their hands. Many games require your child to reach out and grab a floating toy.

Many floating toys are available from online retailers ranging from boats to animals and fish that squirt water. Any floating toys will spark excitement and imaginative play, providing a great distraction from learning to swim.

Some floating toys double as squirters. These can be useful getting your child used to having water on their head when squirted gently. The 'Take A Shower' game on page 87 mentions using a watering can, but a squirting toys will make an excellent substitute instead.

A Google search for 'bath toys' or 'swim toys' should give a wide selection of affordable floating toys.

Egg Flips

Egg flips are simple, lightweight floating toys that are fantastic for building confidence in the water. The object is to blow them over to reveal a different colour and practise breathing in the water at the same

time. Younger children will enjoy trying to grab them as they float around the pool.

A Google search for 'swimming egg flips' will give you a variety of egg flips, including seal and puffer fish-themed flips.

Image courtesy of Complete Leisure
(completeleisure.ie)

'Play is the road to childhood happiness and adult brilliance'
Joseph Pearce

Using Goggles

Using Goggles

Goggles can be used on children from the age of 2, although they are not essential. Using goggles before the age of 2 could slow down progress because we want children to get used to having water in their eyes and become comfortable with the swimming pool environment. Using goggles could prevent this.

The first and most obvious advantage to wearing goggles is that they enable your child to see clearly under the water, enhancing their confidence in putting their faces into the water. Goggles can be a handy tool for encouraging children with a fear of getting their face wet, as you can make the goggles out to be the new 'cool' thing to wear. After putting

their face into the water, the sudden realisation that they can see everything opens up a new world, significantly boosting confidence.

A good reason to wear goggles is the chemicals in the pool water and the sensitivity of children's eyes. Some children are more sensitive to pool water than others, so it is advisable to wear goggles in these circumstances.

Fitting Goggles

Whilst wearing goggles is perfectly safe, putting them on and taking them off can be dangerous, so there are some essential safety points for parents and children to be aware of.

The elastic strap around the back of the head can cause the goggles to snap back if pulled away from the eyes and let go, resulting in injury to the eyes or face. Children should take great care when fitting and removing goggles. Educating them in this area is vital.

The safest way to fit goggles is to get your child to hold the eyes of the goggles onto their own eyes with one hand and then pull the elastic strap over their head with the other. Children can do the opposite when removing the goggles, taking the strap over their heads before removing them from their eyes. Younger children and children who find this difficult should be encouraged to hold the goggles on their eyes with both hands whilst an adult fits or removes the elastic strap.

'Time spent playing with children is never time wasted'
Don Lantero

Introducing Your Baby To Water

Introducing Your Baby To Water

Quality bonding time should be your priority when spending time in the water with your baby.

Introducing your baby to the swimming pool can embed healthy and safe practices and build water confidence early in life. Babies can start being taken into the water at six weeks, although you should ensure they are ready before you begin.

Start in the bathtub

Always ensure a responsible adult supervises your child while they are in the bath. Bath time is the perfect time to teach your child what it is like to be wet, so before introducing your baby to the swimming pool, you can use their bath time to get them used to the water. Filling a cup with water and slowly pouring it over their head is an excellent way for them to experience the feel of water on their face and skin.

When to begin?

The earlier your baby is exposed to the swimming pool, the more confident they will be as a toddler in the water. You can start them in the pool anytime from six weeks old, but only if they have no preexisting medical conditions and are ready. Be sure that umbilical cord or circumcision wounds have healed, and if you have had a C-section, that has healed too. Check with your doctor or health care professional if you are not sure.

What is the ideal water temperature for my baby?

Any clean and well-maintained swimming pool will be fine for your baby's first swimming experience. Still, the temperature of the water is important. The ideal water temperature for babies up to six months old should be around 90°F (32°C). If the pool temperature is below the ideal, keep your swimming session short and closely monitor your baby. Babies can become cold even in a heated pool, so avoid staying too long. If the pool feels too cold for you, it is too cold for your baby.

Your first sessions in the water should last about 10 to 20 minutes, then build up to 30 minutes, the maximum time limit for most babies to be in the water.

If your baby begins to shiver or their lips or fingernails become blue, they are too cold. Do not be alarmed, as this is very common. Remove them from the pool, wrap them in a towel to dry them, and they will soon warm up.

Holding your baby in the water

You must create a relaxed, calm and fun environment when you take your baby into the water, especially for the first time. Your baby will sense any fears or anxieties you may have, and they will also feel the same. Your fear is their fear, so being relaxed and calm is vital.

Enter the pool slowly via the steps so your baby is not shocked by the feel of the water on their skin. Keep your baby pressed against your chest without holding them too tightly.

Once you are in the water, hold your baby under the armpits, ensuring their head is above water, and their face is level with yours. Give them eye contact and smile, showing them what a fun place the swimming pool is to be in.

Supervise your baby at all times

Never take your eyes off of your baby when they are in the water, even if they are playing on the steps or sitting in shallow water splashing about. Hold them at all times or sit in the water next to them or on the steps with them between your legs.

Have some fun!

Start moving your baby around and playing with them once you have both gotten used to the water. Keep smiling and stay relaxed; it will help your baby feel calm and comfortable as they become accustomed to the feeling of the water moving around them.

Try gently bobbing your baby up and down or swirling them back and forth in the water. Float some bath toys in the water, and as they reach for them, hold your baby out horizontally in front of you as though they are swimming. Do not let go of them and ensure their head remains above water.

Submerging your baby

Babies up to six months old have the instinct to hold their breath underwater, and up until the age of three years old, your baby has a reflex that can be used for submerging. The reflex used to condition your baby is a falling reflex. When your baby shuts their eyes, the epiglottis in their throat will close over as well, which then causes them to hold their breath. You must use a verbal cue to teach your baby to use this reflex on cue. Using a clear voice, say the words *'1,2,3 under!'* and engage your baby's reflex. With enough practice, your baby will hear the words *'1,2,3 under!'* and will shut their eyes on cue, and that is when they are ready to submerge.

Alena Sarri of Aquatots explains that to condition your baby to engage this reflex on cue, use a wet hand, washcloth or a small amount of water in a bucket or cup. Use the cue *'1,2,3 under!'* gently wipe or pour the water over your baby's face. Eventually, your baby will hear the words and shut their eyes on cue. This conditioning can be started from birth.

You must allow your baby to learn the cue and engage the reflex before you attempt submerging. Waiting until your baby is ready will mean the outcome will be a comfortable, relaxed swimmer.

According to Sarri, once your baby has learnt the verbal cue, it is time to move on to submerging. Remember that your baby has two cues: the verbal (*1,2,3 under!*) and a physical cue, which is a small lift on the word 'under'. You must hold your child horizontally in the water as a vertical submersion will push the water up their nose, and this stings. Move with your baby; ensure you can see their face, and use the verbal cue, lift on the word under, and if your baby shuts their eyes, they are ready to submerge. Focus on your baby's eyes, not their mouth. If their eyes are closed, the airway will be as well, so even if their mouth is open, the water can not get passed the throat.

At this point, you will also need to read your baby's face and body language to ensure they are relaxed and ready for the submersion. If your baby's body seems tight, or they are straining to keep their head up, or saying or making no sounds or gestures, please DO NOT submerge. Allow your baby to ease in and relax with what you are about to do. All your movements when submerging your baby must be smooth and controlled.

Try to use natural movement and not force your child through the water. Babies under the age of three do not have enough neck strength to hold their head forward against the force of the water, so when forcing or pushing through, their head will tip back, and the water will go up their nose, which stings. Fast and sudden movements also tend to startle and frighten babies. When a baby is startled, they throw their arms outwards and breathe in. If this happens underwater, your baby will not only be shocked and unhappy, but they will have had a big gulp of water. Making your movements gentle and smooth will be paramount to your baby enjoying their time under the water.

Games to play with your baby

The games in this book have been created for children who can understand instructions. Therefore, many babies may not understand the concept of an activity or game. Still, there is no reason why you cannot adapt the learning aim of the game to suit your baby. For example, when bright floating toys are placed in front of a baby, they will naturally reach out to take them. Also, as they develop, they can mimic sounds and actions. Blowing bubbles in front of them and making noises as you swim them across the surface of the water will help encourage them to feel comfortable in the water.

Nursery rhymes and singing

Babies typically respond well to having songs sung to them, particularly nursery rhymes. They create a sense of calm and reassurance, especially if it is a song that your baby is familiar with, having it sung to them on other occasions.

Nursery rhymes that climax in you submerging your baby are also popular. For example, *'Humpty Dumpty - had a great fall'* or *'Ring-a-ring-a-roses. We all fall down'.* Songs like these can bring fun to your time in the water. A word of caution, however. If your baby is distressed, the song will increase their anxiety at the anticipation of being submerged. Only use songs for this purpose if your baby is happy with being submerged.

'Life is more fun if you play games'
Roald Dahl

Entering The Water

Entering the Water

For the non-swimmer, entering the water can be either hugely daunting or very exciting. Either way, children must do it safely and appropriately. Teach your child to use the following entries accordingly:

Stepping in using the poolside steps

Entering via the pool's steps is the best entry for the nervous non-swimmer. Encourage your child to hold the rails with both hands and step down one step at a time. This safe and gradual entry allows them to take their time.

The sitting swivel entry

This entry is the safest and works best on deck-level swimming pools.

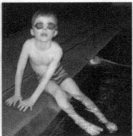

From a sitting position, with legs in the water, show your child how to place both hands to one side and turn their backs to the water. They should then lower themselves gradually into the water, keeping hold of the poolside.

Jumping Entry

Before using a jumping entry, you should always consider the water's depth compared to your child's size. They should start with their toes over the edge of the poolside, jump away from the poolside and bend their knees on landing. This entry is best for more confident children and should always be in water of a depth they can stand up.

Open your mind and get creative!

The names and themes of the games outlined in this book are just suggestions. You know your child better than anyone else. Therefore, you know their interests and current characters, toys and tv programmes that will spark their excitement. For example, instead of *'Rocket Launch' (p98)*, they could be their favourite toy character diving across the sky or a unicorn stretching through the clouds. Instead of *'Pop Ups' (p88)*, they could pretend to be playing peek-a-boo with their favourite toys.

Use your imagination to set the scene, the characters and whatever ignites your child's interest. You cannot go wrong if you keep the **learning aim** and the **swimming skill** at the heart of the game. As your child becomes immersed in their fantasy world, they will learn the essential basics of swimming without knowing they are doing so.

Getting Used To The Water

Movement Through the Water

During the early stages of learning to swim, it is essential that children get used to the water slowly and gradually and, to a certain degree, at their own pace. Simple movements through the water, such as walking or sliding their feet, are excellent confidence builders. Children should be encouraged to move around using their arms and hands whilst walking to get a 'feel' for the water.

Some children may require floats or buoyancy aids to support them while moving through the water and it will be more common in the nervous child. Buoyancy aids should be discouraged as soon as confidence builds before they become dependent on them.

Movement patterns can take the form of shapes made on the pool floor with the feet, changes of direction, and collecting a floating object such as a ball. As confidence builds further, pupils can hop, skip and jump.

1. Monkey Around

Skill: moving in the water

Aim: to get used to being in the water and partially submerging.

Difficulty: ★

Equipment: none

This activity works best in pools where the water level is below deck level; however, a deck-level pool will work also. Have your child hold onto the poolside or pool rail with both hands like a monkey hanging from bars. They then lower themselves into the water to a comfortable depth without letting go. They then raise themselves again like a monkey pulling themselves up. They repeat this movement, gradually lowering themselves deeper into the water each time. They can also move along the poolside with each up-and-down movement as if monkeying around!

Key phrases: *'pull yourself along' 'see how low you can go'*

Progression: change hands as they move along, lowering themselves with one hand holding the poolside. Have them lower themselves so that their chin and mouth becomes submerged.

2. Wave Machine

Skill: moving in the water

Aim: to get used to moving in the water and making the water move.

Difficulty: ★

Equipment: none

The ideal depth to play this game is with the water level around chest level. Your child starts facing the poolside and holds the wall firmly with both hands. They then push themselves back until their arms are straight and pull themselves inwards towards the wall again. This repeated movement causes the water to form waves in front and behind them. The faster and more vigorous their back-and-forth movements, the bigger the waves they make.

Key phrases: *'push harder, pull harder' 'see how big you can make the waves'*

Progression: perform the wave machine action with their chin or mouth submerged. See if they can make the waves splash their face.

3. Slide And Ski

Skill: moving through the water.

Aim: to get used to moving through the water independently.

Difficulty: ★

Equipment: none

This game is excellent for getting your child moving independently and confidently through the water, as they can play it in any depth of water up to chest level. From a standing position, they move forward through the pool by sliding their feet one at a time across the pool floor. They can slide in a diagonal movement as if they are skiing. They can play this without needing to lift their feet from the pool floor, which is helpful for the nervous child or child that lacks balance.

Key phrases: *'take your time, slowly at first' 'keep your feet on the floor' 'small movements, then make them bigger'*

Progression: place objects on the pool floor for your child to seek out and collect. If the water becomes too deep for them to reach, they may have to use some breath-holding and submersion skills to retrieve them.

4. Quack Quack!

Skill: moving through the water

Aim: to move through the water in a partially submerged position using the arms as necessary.

Difficulty: ★ ★

Equipment: none

The object of this game is to pretend to be a duck moving through the water. Have your child squat down under the water so that their shoulders are submerged. They walk through the water using small steps, lifting their feet off the floor. They may need to use small arm movements to help pull them forwards and, of course, use appropriate duck noises as they move through the water.

Key phrases: *'small steps' 'pull back with your arms to help you move' 'keep your chin on the water'*

Progression: blow bubbles across the water surface or submerge the face to collect objects from the pool floor.

5. Frogger

Skill: moving around in the water

Aim: to use a jumping action to gain confidence in moving around in the water.

Difficulty: ★ ★

Equipment: none

Have your child stand with their knees bent and shoulders under the water. They then start to jump, using small jumps at first, making them bigger and bigger as their confidence grows. They may have to use their arms in a downward motion to help them to jump and to balance. Using this frog-like action to jump several times without pause may cause them to fall forwards, so you may prefer to use buoyancy aids or have some support standing by. Getting used to this jumping and falling action will boost their confidence hugely.

Key phrases: *'use your arms to help you jump' 'jump as high as you can'*

Progression: completely submerge after each jump

6. Fetch

Skill: moving around in the water

Aim: to increase confidence by moving around the pool in different directions.

Difficulty: ★ ★

Equipment: floating toys

Place a ball or similar floating object a distance from your child and have them fetch it. You can role-play them being a dog and you being their owner and have them go *'fetch!'* on your command. They then walk, run or move through the water however they wish to collect the object and return it to you. They can use their arms and hands to help balance and move faster. Consider the distance they have to travel to retrieve the object and ensure that it is achievable without them but challenging without them becoming despondent.

Key phrases: *'use long strides' 'use your arms to go faster' 'reach for it'*

Progression: use multiple objects and have your child collect them in a particular order or within a specific time. Have them collect the object using only a few steps or strides.

7. Control The Ball

Skill: moving around in the water

Aim: to increase confidence by moving around the pool in different directions.

Difficulty: ★ ★

Equipment: ball

Using a football or similar size ball, your child uses their body to manoeuvre it around the pool. They walk around in water using their chest, chin or another body part, depending on the water depth, to push the ball around. They can control it from one set point to another or around in a course or pattern set out by you. They use their arms and hands to help them move and change direction, not control the ball.

Key phrases: *'use your hands to control your movement'*

Progression: use their head to control the ball or manoeuvre it around a course within a specific time.

8. Steer The Speed Boat

Skill: moving through the water and breathing

Aim: to move in different directions through the water while breathing.

Difficulty: ★ ★

Equipment: float or kickboard, floating objects

Your child can play this game in shallow water, where they hold a float out in front of them and steer it like a speed boat. Have them lower themselves to the water level and blow bubbles as they navigate the boat, making engine noises at the same time. You could use objects placed on the water for the boat to collect or as a course for the boat to steer around.

Key phrases: *'keep your chin on the water' 'take a deep breath and blow' 'make bubbles like an engine'*

Progression: collect objects from under the water by taking a deep breath and submerging.

Breathing

Breathing Techniques

When getting used to the water and learning to swim, the ability to breathe can be a fear that holds children back. You want your child to become a confident, competent swimmer, so they need to be able to breathe out in the water, control their breathing and be comfortable with water around their face, mouth, and nose.

Breathing is an involuntary action that happens automatically as we go about our everyday lives and therefore requires no conscious thought. So, children would never have given it a single thought. However, breathing becomes a conscious, physical act that can cause significant stress for some children when performing activities in and under the water.

Teach your child to hold their breath

If holding their breath is difficult for your child, have them pretend they are about to blow out the candles on their birthday cake. Explain and demonstrate that they take a deep breath before they blow them out. Show them what this looks like, then explain that they only have to breathe in, not blow out. Exaggerate your demonstration by taking a huge deep breath, puffing out your chest and pointing to your tightly closed mouth to show that you are *'holding it all in'*.

Trickle Breathing

Trickle breathing is the most commonly used breathing technique in swimming because it is controlled and efficient. Teaching your child trickle breathing will pay huge dividends when they come to learn basic swimming strokes.

Trickle breathing is the simple act of inhaling, slowly exhaling, and controlling the speed of the exhale. Encourage your child to take a huge breath in and then blow it out 'through pursed lips' as if they are *'blowing bubbles through a straw in a drink'*. They can practice this technique anywhere at any time, but in the pool is where it is most effective. Have them blow out slowly across the surface of the water so they can experience the bubbles tickling their nose while they control their breath.

The 'slow puncture' game (p59) is the best for learning and developing trickle breathing.

Children who are new or nervous about swimming can become distressed or anxious about putting their face in the water or blowing bubbles. Therefore breathing practices must be developed progressively and at your child's pace. You should never force them to undertake an activity or pour water over their face without them being made aware.

Teaching practices:
- cupping water in the hands and then wetting the face
- blowing bubbles across the surface of the water
- blowing a toy or ball across the surface of the water
- submerging the body under the water to collect a partially or fully submerged object
- practising at home in the bathroom

9. Blow It Away

Skill: breathing

Aim: gain confidence in blowing water and having water around the mouth.

Difficulty: ★

Equipment: none

This activity requires your child to scoop water into their hands and blow it away. Have them cup their hands to hold as much water as possible. If they find this tricky, demonstrate it, or use your hands as their cup. They then bring their chin towards their hands and blow gently until they get used to the water splashing around their mouth.

Key phrases: *'breath in through your mouth' 'take a big deep breath' 'blow out through your lips'*

Progression: blow vigorously to cause a more explosive reaction, or place their lips into the cupped water and blow out.

10. Blow It Along

Skill: Breathing

Aim: to learn a basic breathing technique and gain confidence in breathing and moving around the pool.

Difficulty: ★

Equipment: a light floating object such as a small ball or an egg flip

Have your child crouch down in shallow water or a water depth with their chin on the surface of the water. They walk around the pool, blowing a floating object along. You could set a predetermined destination for the object, such as the poolside or another floating object.

Key phrases: *'take a deep breath and blow' 'keep your chin on the water' 'let the water tickle your chin'*

Progression: race your child with another object over a set distance or have them complete a course within a specified time. These will create a sense of urgency and speed, which may distract them from any fears or anxieties about breathing.

11. Slow Puncture

Skill: breathing

Aim: to learn and develop breath control.

Difficulty: ★ ★

Equipment: none

This game involves breathing out into the water very slowly. Explain to your child that they are pretending to be an inflatable object such as a tyre, ring or an inflatable toy with a hole in and, therefore, a slow puncture. Have them take a deep breath and inflate their lungs as much as possible. They then let the air out very slowly through their tightly pursed lips, as if the puncture is deflating them. You can time how long they can make their breath last before it runs out. The longer, the better.

Key phrases: *'take in a huge deep breath' 'breathe out slowly' 'keep your lips tight' 'make your breath last as long as you can'*

Progression: gradually submerge the mouth, nose, and eventually the eyes before completely submerging.

12. *Name That Sound*

Skill: breathing

Aim: to learn a basic breathing technique and gain confidence in breathing into the water.

Difficulty: ★ ★

Equipment: none

This game uses a trickle breathing technique (exhaling in a controlled way through the mouth) and can be played in any water depth. You and your child take turns blowing out into the water for this game. You can blow out slowly, with force or in any other imaginative way that creates an unusual sound. The idea is to have a particular sound in mind, and they must guess what the sound is, for example, a speed boat, an animal or a machine. Take turns guessing each other's sounds.

Key phrases: *'take a deep breath in' 'blow across the surface' 'let the bubbles tickle your nose'*

Progression: allow the nose to submerge as they blow and progress onto the eyes if confidence allows.

13. Fishing Boats

Skill: Breathing and submerging

Aim: to develop a breathing technique and gain confidence in submerging.

Difficulty: ★ ★ ★

Equipment: none

Your child moves around the pool like a fishing boat looking for fish. They could blow bubbles across the water and make the boat noise as they do so. On your command, *'fish!'*, they quickly take a breath and submerge their face into the water as if collecting some fish before recovering and continuing their journey.

Key phrases: *'blow out gently' 'deep breathing and dive down'*

Progression: have them reach down and collect an object from the pool floor, if shallow enough or from your hand, held under the water. Use multiple objects to increase the time submerged.

14. Sinking Scuba Diver

Skill: submerging and breathing

Aim: to gain confidence in submerging completely and using a controlled breathing technique.

Difficulty: ★ ★ ★

Equipment: none

In water around chest depth, have your child take a deep breath, bend their knees and slowly submerge. As they sink, they slowly exhale and watch the bubbles rise, like a sinking scuba diver. Seeing how long they can make their bubbles last by continually blowing out is a great way to learn how to control their breath.

Key phrases: *'take a huge deep breath' 'sink slowly' 'slowly blow your bubbles'*

Progression: sit on the pool floor and see how long they can remain there.

Regaining A Standing Position

Regaining a standing position

Learning how to stand up mid-swim is a huge confidence booster. As long as your child is in the water of standing depth, being able to stop and stand up can often smooth out any nerves or anxieties.

Children often find their way of stopping and standing up mid-swim; if they do, there is no need to spend much time refining the technique explained here. If they are confident and can regain a standing position without undue stress, let them do it their way.

Children can hold the poolside and use it as a starting point to learn the basic movements needed to regain standing. They can progress to using floats or buoyancy aids. As confidence grows, your child can attempt standing without assistance, requiring more effective use of the arms and hands. They can also progress to a moving exercise, moving first towards and then away from the poolside.

An explanation of the technique is detailed here in case you need to demonstrate it.

The movement should be smooth and relaxed as they use their arms to pull downwards and backwards, bringing their knees forward as they lift their head and place their feet on the pool floor.

Hands and arms draw down and knees are drawn forwards and upwards

Hands pull backwards as the head lifts and the feet are placed on the pool floor

When standing up from a supine (face up) position, the movements should again be smooth and relaxed as their pull upwards and forwards, bring their knees forwards, lift their head and place their feet on the pool floor.

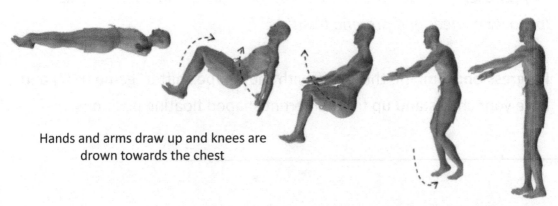

Hands and arms draw up and knees are drown towards the chest

Hands pull upwards as the head lifts and the feet are placed on the pool floor

15. Skydiver Landing

Skill: standing up mid swim

Aim: to regain a standing position from a static floating position.

Difficulty: ★

Equipment: none

This game is best played in water around chest depth and can be played with buoyancy aids if your child needs them. Have your child adopt a floating position on their front in the shape of a star, with arms and legs spread out wide. On your countdown, *'3, 2, 1...touchdown'*, your child pulls down with their arms, bends their knees towards their chest and places their feet on the pool floor like a skydiver using their parachute to come into land.

Key phrases: *'pull down and back with both arms' 'lift your head up' 'bend your knees and pretend to sit'*

Progression: combine this game with the 'shape shifter' game (p77) and have your child stand up from different shaped floating positions.

16. Rocket Landing

Skill: standing up mid-swim

Aim: to learn the movements needed to stop mid-swim and regain a standing position from a face down position.

Difficulty: ★ ★

Equipment: none

The ideal water depth for this game is around shoulder depth. Have your child start with one foot against the wall and one foot on the pool floor. They push away from the poolside like a rocket taking off and glide momentarily across the surface before *'coming into land'* as they stop and place both feet on the pool floor.

Encourage your child to pull downwards with their arms whilst bringing their knees forward before placing both feet on the floor.

Key phrases: *'pull down and back with both arms' 'lift your head up' 'bend your knees and pretend to sit'*

Progression: have your child perform this without buoyancy aids or with their face submerged.

17. Ejector Seat Landing

Skill: standing up mid-swim

Aim: to learn the movements needed to stop when swimming on the back and regain a standing position.

Difficulty: ★ ★

Equipment: none

The ideal water depth for this game is around shoulder depth. Have your child hold the poolside with both hands and feet against the wall. They push away from the poolside as if being ejected like a pilot and glide momentarily across the surface before *'coming into land'* or *'parachuting down'* as they stop and place both feet on the pool floor.

Encourage your child to pull upwards with their arms whilst bringing their knees forward and to sit up before placing both feet on the floor.

Key phrases: *'pull down and back with both arms' 'lift your head up' 'bend your knees and pretend to sit'*

Progression: have your child roll onto their front before stopping and standing up.

Floating And Buoyancy

69

The psychology of floating

It is typical for beginners who fear water to think that the water is pulling them down. As a parent or carer, showing your child that the water is trying to support them is essential. The human body does not sink like a stone. Those that do not naturally float usually sink slowly and gradually.

So with that in mind, we must encourage children to move their arms and legs to help the water support them. Those movements can be very subtle and small, and they may have to be more significant movements to help generate some momentum.

Either way, you must encourage your child to do their bit to help the water support them.

What if they naturally sink?

The simple facts are that fat floats and muscle sinks. Therefore generally, fat people are better floaters than thin or muscular people.

Generally speaking, our legs are heavy and therefore sink. Our upper body will tend to float because our lungs contain air. But, the higher our body fat percentage, the better our chance of naturally staying afloat.

However, a lean child with a low body fat percentage can remain at the surface of the water as they swim, despite the fact that their body naturally wants to sink.

18. Seahorses

Skill: floating

Aim: to get used to moving around the pool without touching or standing on the pool floor.

Difficulty: ★

Equipment: pool noodle/woggle

Your child plays this game in an upright vertical position with a pool noodle between their legs (like riding a bicycle). One end of the noodle comes up in front of them, while the other is behind them like a tail. Without touching the pool floor, they use their legs in a cycling-type action to move around the pool like a seahorse.

Key phrases: *'use your legs to move around the pool' 'feel the water around you'*

Progression: using arms to paddle and blowing bubbles at the surface of the water.

19. Soaring Eagle

Skill: floating

Aim: use floats to gain confidence in lifting feet off the floor and floating.

Difficulty: ★

Equipment: floats or kickboards

This game uses floats or kickboards to help your child build confidence in lifting their feet off of the pool floor. Have them place a float under each arm and begin with one foot on the pool floor. They gently lay forward and use the support of the floats to help lift their foot off the floor and *'soar like an eagle'* with the floats as wings. You will need to support and assist your child with the movement and floating position until they gain enough confidence to soar like an eagle independently.

Key phrases: *'relax and take your time' 'let the water support you' 'glide through the air like an eagle'*

Progression: take a deep breath and look down as if the eagle is looking for their prey.

20. Star Gazing

Skill: floating

Aim: to gain confidence in a floating supine (face up) position.

Difficulty: ★ ★

Equipment: none

This activity can be performed with your child using buoyancy aids as needed. Alternatively, you can provide manual support by placing the palm of one hand under the back of their head. Have your child lay face up in the water with arms and legs stretched outwards, adopting a star shape. Encourage them to look upwards to the stars.

Key phrases: *'look up at the stars' 'push your chest and hips up to the surface' 'let the water support you'*

Progression: gradually reduce the amount of manual support and allow them to float independently.

21. Floating Stars

Skill: floating

Aim: to gain confidence in lifting the feet off the pool floor and floating.

Difficulty: ★ ★

Equipment: woggle if needed

Your child can play this game with buoyancy aids (the ideal aid is a woggle) or without buoyancy aids. Your child begins with shoulders submerged and arms stretched out in front and wide apart. Standing on one leg, they stretch the other out behind, lift the standing leg off the pool floor, and lay into a star float position. How long can they maintain this floating position?

Key Phrases: *'relax and take your time' 'stretch out like a big star' 'let the water support you'*

Progression: play this without buoyancy aids if they have used them previously. Have your child play this with face down, blowing bubbles.

22. Mushroom Float

Skill: floating

Aim: to gain confidence in breath holding and to float in a stationary position.

Difficulty: ★ ★ ★

Equipment: none

This activity requires your child to adopt a tucked position, with knees against their chest and arms wrapped around their legs, holding the tucked shape. Have them take a deep breath and hold it in as they adopt the tucked position with their chin on their chest and face submerged. As they float, their body will roll into place with their rounded back just above the surface of the water, looking like the top of a mushroom. See how long they can hold this floating position.

Key phrases: *'take a deep breath' 'hold your knees onto your chest' 'tuck your chin on your chest' 'float as long as you can'*

Progression: have them stretch out and then reform the tucked mushroom shape without resurfacing.

23. Shape Shifter

Skill: floating

Aim: to become comfortable with floating in different positions, including face up and face down.

Difficulty: ★ ★ ★

Equipment: pool noodle/woggle

The best way to play this game is in shoulder-depth water. Use a pool noodle under the arms (or a float under each arm) and have your child create different shapes with their body without touching the pool floor. They can create shapes in an upright position, to begin with, such as star shapes, 'pencil' shapes and tuck positions. When your child becomes more confident, they can create shapes in a prone (face down) or supine (face up) position. On your command, *'shape shift!'*, they change shape and see how long they can hold the position for.

Key phrases: *'relax and take your time' 'stretch out' 'let your body come to the surface'*

Progression: switch between floating shapes on the front and the back. Alternating between face down and face up will boost confidence. Remove buoyancy aids as necessary.

24. Pancake Flipping

Skill: floating

Aim: to gain confidence in moving between a face-up and face-down floating position.

Difficulty: ★ ★ ★

Equipment: none

This game requires confidence in floating and is best played without buoyancy aids. Have your child adopt a floating position, such as a star shape, face upwards with arms and legs wide and eyes looking skyward. Have them pretend they are a pancake cooking in a pan, and on your command, *'flip!'*, they flip over onto their front and into a face-down star float. Repeat the flip command as often as you want and see how long they can maintain their floating positions.

Key phrases: *'relax and take your time' 'eyes to the sky' 'take a deep breath and hold it all in' 'stretch out and feel the water supporting you'*

Progression: keep them in a face-down position for a few seconds longer to help with breath control.

Submerging

Underwater Confidence

The ability to submerge the face is arguably one of the most critical stages of learning to swim.

Water immersion for the first time is a new experience for many individuals, and fear, lack of confidence or uncertainty are normal feelings. If your child shows any of these feelings, it is essential not to force them into anything. Some children will find getting their face wet and submerging easy, but it will be terrifying for others. You know your child better than anyone, but a gentle and gradual approach is needed if they are anxious or fearful.

Below are some steps to work through to teach your child how to hold their breath and submerge. Proceed to the next stage only when your child is happy.

Stage 1: Getting the face wet

Remember: getting the face wet and splashing in the face are two completely different concepts. The effects on children are not always positive.

Here are a few activities to work through:

Blowing bubbles on the surface of the water or blowing an object along as they swim is a great way to build confidence at this stage. Encourage your child to blow gently, like blowing through a straw, or blow with force, like blowing out candles on a cake.

Cupping water in their own hands and throwing it onto their face can further build confidence. This activity works with a friend because it can encourage an anxious child to copy their friend. You can demonstrate it yourself and make light of it by making it look like a fun thing to do.

Throwing and catching a ball is an excellent distraction from the splashes of water. Making the ball land in front of your child can result in a wet face without them realising it. The smallest splashes from the softest throws will be sufficient to have a positive effect.

Stage 2: Partially submerging the face

Partial submersion is also best achieved with a gradual approach.

Firstly, you must teach your child how to hold their breath by *'breathing in and holding it all in'*. Some children will be able to do this quickly, and others will learn by trial and error as they partially submerge their faces and realise they cannot breathe underwater! Whatever the outcome, as a parent, you must proceed with caution and, at the same time, enforce a fun learning environment to distract your child from potential discomfort and distress.

Don't blow out the candles!

If holding their breath is difficult for your child, have them pretend they are about to blow out the candles on their birthday cake. Explain and demonstrate that they take a deep breath before they blow them out. Show them what this looks like, then explain that they only have to breathe in, not blow out. Exaggerate your demonstration by taking a huge deep breath, puffing out your chest and pointing to your tightly closed mouth to show that you are *'holding it all in'*.

An object can then be placed just under the surface of the water, shallow enough for your child to see and reach for it but deep enough to submerge the mouth to get it. Once they have gained confidence with this exercise, you can lower the object slightly to encourage their mouth and nose to be submerged.

Stage 3: Total Submersion

Stage 2 naturally leads quickly onto stage 3, where you place the object below the water surface. Encourage your child to retrieve it by completely submerging their head underwater. By this stage, breath-holding should be more accomplished, and your child should begin to relax more as they get used to immersing and become more confident.

Fearful and tearful

Many children are fearful at the thought of going under the water. Fear does not affect all children, but try to be ready for it in case yours is affected. The golden rule here is never to rush them into an experience they are not ready for. However, resistance does necessarily mean that they aren't ready. Always show empathy and understanding and never be pushy or force it. When they eventually take the plunge, embrace and congratulate them with a big hug. Let them calm down, then ask specific questions. Was it fun? Was it scary? Sometimes even children who experience a lot of upset also find the experience fun.

Okay, or too much?

When deciding whether it is upsetting but *okay* or is it *too much*, there are a few questions to ask yourself. How quickly does your child recover from their upset? Do they want to stay in the pool? Is the pool still a fun place for them to play? If the upset continues, your child leaves the pool and refuses to return, or if they suddenly see the pool as not a nice place, each one signals that the underwater experience was too much. In this case, the best course of action is to back off. Repeat some of the fun things you and your child did and build the fun and trust back into the whole swimming pool experience.

The dangers of overconfidence

You and your child have worked hard to master breathing and submerging. Now, suddenly you discover that your child not only does it, but they do it comfortably and even playfully. This is a sign that your child has become overconfident. Look out for that moment when they put their head and face under the water voluntarily and constantly during play. Being underwater has gone from a scary place to a fun place. This is when we must pay the most attention. Why? Because their comfort can lead to moments where they swallow water and choke. We need to be right there, watching closely. We have to resist the urge to get overly relaxed at this stage because they will not be able to resist the urge to have fun in overconfidence.

25. Wash Your Face

Skill: submerging

Aim: to get used to being splashed and having a wet face.

Difficulty: ★

Equipment: none

In water of standing depth, have your child cup both hands together, scoop up the water and use it to wash their face. Have them repeat this as many times as they want. Encourage them to close their eyes, and when they become more confident, encourage them to open their eyes sooner. As the water runs off their face, encourage them to blink their eyes rather than rub it away with their hands.

Key phrases: *'use lots of water' 'keep washing!' 'blink your eyes, and the water will go away'*

Progression: splash the water faster and more vigorously or take a deep breath and place their face down into the water to wash.

26. Take A Shower

Skill: submerging

Aim: to get used to water pouring over the head and down the face.

Equipment: sponge, squirter or toy watering can (if available)

Difficulty: ★

This game is similar to the *'Wash Your Face'* game as it involves the face and head getting wet. This time you pour water over their head and allow it to run down their face as if they are taking a shower. They can use their hands to cup and pour the water, or you can pour for them. Encourage them to close their eyes and hold their breath before you shower them. To add to the effect, you could use a sponge, a squirting toy or a toy watering can if available.

Key phrases: *'hold your breath' 'let the water run down' 'blink your eyes, and the water will go away'*

Progression: use a larger container to pour more water or pour the water slowly to make the shower last longer.

27. Pop Ups

Skill: submerging

Aim: to gain confidence in gradually submerging the face.

Difficulty: ★

Equipment: none

Standing in shallow water, around chest depth, encourage your child to sink down and then, on your command, *'pop up!'.* This game is an excellent way to get them used to holding their breath and submerging their face. The nervous child only needs to submerge their mouth. As confidence grows, they can progress to mouth, nose, eyes, and finally complete submersion. Encourage them to bend their knees as they sink so they can spring up fast like a Jack-in-a-box.

Key phrases: *'relax and take your time' 'hold your breath and slowly sink' 'feel the water around your mouth and nose'*

Progression: keep them under the water for longer before you shout *'pop up!'* to help them hold their breath slightly longer.

28. How Many Fingers?

Skill: submerging

Aim: to learn how to submerge with eyes open

Difficulty: ★ ★

Equipment: none

You can play this game in shallow water, and your child can play it wearing goggles. It is a simple game of counting fingers underwater. Your child can begin by taking a deep breath and looking down from the surface of the water. You hold up a certain number of fingers under the water for them to count and let you know how many. As they become more confident, have them submerge their face and head completely before holding up your fingers for them to count.

Key phrases: *'relax and take your time' 'take a deep breath and hold it all in'*

Progression: display your fingers under the water one finger at a time to encourage your child to remain underwater slightly longer.

29. Lucky Dip

Skill: submerging

Aim: to gain confidence in holding the breath and submerging the face.

Difficulty: ★ ★

Equipment: a selection of toys

To play this game, you will need a selection of small toys. They do not have to be sinkers, but they have to be small enough for you to be able to hold three or four of them in your hands under the water. Your child is then encouraged to hold their breath, reach down and take one out of your hand. This is an excellent game for children anxious about submerging their faces. You can help by adjusting the level at which you hold the toys. You can hold them depending on their confidence level, so they only have to dip their mouth or mouth and nose. Gradually increase the depth as their confidence grows.

Key phrases: *'relax and take your time' 'reach down and see what you can find' 'take a deep breath, hold it all in'*

Progression: have your child take more than one object or have objects in both hands and place them far apart.

30. Catch It Quick!

Skill: submerging

Aim: to gain confidence in completely submerging underwater

Difficulty: ★ ★ ★

Equipment: sinkers

Depending on your child's confidence level, this game can be played in any water depth. It is recommended that they wear goggles. The game's object is for your child to catch a sinking object before it reaches the bottom of the pool. Depending on your child's ability and confidence level, you can make this easy or difficult. The first step is to hold a sinker just under the surface of the water. Your child takes a deep breath, and on your command, *'1,2,3...catch!'*, you let it go. Your child then submerges to catch the object. You can modify the game by changing the object for a heavier one that sinks faster.

Key phrases: *'take a deep breath and hold it all in'* *'sink as fast as you can'*

Progression: get your child to catch multiple sinkers in one breath before they land on the pool floor.

31. Deep Sea Diver

Skill: submerging

Aim: to develop submerging skills and become confident with complete submersion.

Difficulty: ★ ★ ★

Equipment: sinkers

This game is similar to 'Catch It Quick', in that your child has to submerge underwater to collect objects. This time they are on the pool floor. The depth of water you choose to play this in will determine the difficulty level, so have your child's ability in mind when you set this game up. Have your child pretend they are a deep sea diver. They could be looking for a shipwreck, sea life or treasure. To make the game more interesting, you could allocate points for specific objects and see what score they can get in a certain number of dives.

Key phrases: *'take a big deep breath' 'head down, bottom up' 'stretch down to the bottom'*

Progression: place the objects further apart and have your child collect more than one per dive down.

Gliding

Gliding

Gliding, from a swimming point of view, is floating through the water, either at the surface or underwater, without assistance or movement from the arms or legs. It usually begins with a forceful push from the poolside or solid edge to generate some propulsion.

A streamlined body shape is essential for a glide to gain and maintain some distance.

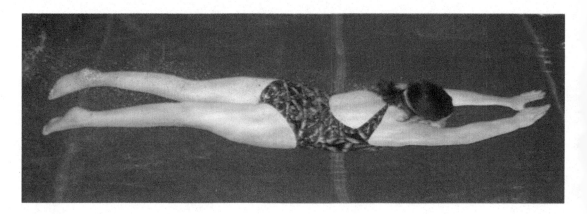

For a glide through the water to be efficient and effective, hands and feet must be together to create a pointed streamlined shape. This will allow the body to cut through the water easily. If your child's hands and feet are apart, their body shape will be wide, creating resistance and making the glide ineffective.

The gliding games in this section have been designed to encourage your child to adopt a streamlined body shape whilst developing their gliding and floating confidence.

32. Sail The Raft

Skill: gliding

Aim: to build confidence in gliding across the surface of the water.

Difficulty: ★

Equipment: float or kickboard

This activity is performed in water that your child can stand in. Your child holds a float or kickboard in both hands out in front with their arms straight and pretends it is a raft. They push off from the poolside or pool floor and stretch out into a glide, with the float providing some support. Smaller children and children with lower confidence will need additional support from you.

Key phrases: *'stretch out' 'make your body long and thin' 'stretch the raft across the water'*

Progression: have your child perform the glide whilst blowing bubbles into the water or submerging their face.

33. Floating Away

Skill: floating

Aim: to gain confidence in gliding in a supine (face up) position.

Difficulty: ★ ★

Equipment: floats or kickboards

Depending on your child's confidence level, this activity can be performed with one or two floats. They can hold a float under each arm, to begin with. Have them adopt a flat floating position with hips and chest high and legs and feet together. With your assistance, guide them as they float along the surface of the water.

Key phrases: *'stretch out' 'feel the water supporting you' 'relax and float along'*

Progression: use one float held across the chest or have your child glide along without any buoyancy aids.

34. Torpedo

Skill: gliding

Aim: to learn how to adopt a streamlined position and travel through the water

Difficulty: ★ ★

Equipment: none

This game is about how far your child can stretch and glide across the surface of the water. Children can play this in shallow or deep water, with assistance if needed. Have your child start with one foot against the wall and one foot on the pool floor (if in shallow water). You count down '5, 4, 3, 2, 1...torpedo!' They push away from the poolside like a rocket taking off and glide across the surface, seeing how far they can travel.

Children can wear buoyancy aids for this game, but be aware that some aids can cause resistance, slow the glide, and be counterproductive.

Key phrases: *'stretch out' 'make your body long and thin' 'keep your hands and feet together'.*

Progression: play the game without any buoyancy aids if your child has used them previously. Push off and glide with face and head tucked down between their stretched out arms.

35. Rocket Launch

Skill: gliding

Aim: to learn how to adopt a streamlined position and travel through the water in a supine (on the back) position

Difficulty: ★ ★

Equipment: floats or kickboards

Like 'Torpedo', this game is about how far your child can stretch and glide across the surface of the water. Children can play this in shallow or deep water, with assistance if needed. Have your child start by holding the poolside with both hands, in a tucked position, with their back to the water and with both feet foot against the pool wall. You count down '5, 4, 3, 2, 1...blast off!' They push away from the poolside like a rocket taking off and glide across the surface, seeing how far they can travel.

Children can wear buoyancy aids for this game, but be aware that some aids can cause resistance, slow the glide, and be counterproductive.

Key phrases: *'stretch out' 'make your body long and thin' 'keep your arms by your sides' 'look up to the sky'*

Progression: play the game without any buoyancy aids if your child has used them previously. Push off and glide with arms stretched out on either side of the head.

36. Superhero Glides

Skill: gliding and standing

Aim: to develop a streamlined body position and regain a standing position.

Difficulty: ★ ★ ★

Equipment: none

This game is similar to *'Torpedo'*, but with regaining a standing position at the end of the glide. The game is best played in water of standing depth and tests how far your child can stretch and glide across the surface of the water. Your child has to pretend that they are their favourite superhero or character. They push away from the poolside like a superhero flying through the air. As their glide slows and stops, they come to land by pulling down with their arms, bending their knees upwards and placing their feet on the pool floor.

Key phrases: *'stretch out' 'make your body long and thin' 'pull down with your arms to stand up'*

Progression: have your child roll onto their back as the glide slows, and then stand up from a supine (on the back) position.

37. Sausage Roll

Skill: gliding

Aim: to maintain a streamlined glide whilst rolling over.

Difficulty: ★ ★ ★

Equipment: none

This game is also based on *'Torpedo'* but requires your child to roll onto their back as they glide away from the poolside. Have your child push away from the poolside into a stretched-out, streamlined position. They pretend they are a sausage turning on the grill as they maintain their streamlined body position. Your child can also begin by gliding on their back and then *'sausage roll'* onto their front.

Key phrases: *'keep your hands and feet together' 'stay stretched out and long' '*

Progression: roll over again into their original starting position whilst maintaining the glide.

38. Cork Screw

Skill: gliding

Aim: to maintain a streamlined glide whilst performing a continuous rolling motion.

Difficulty: ★ ★ ★

Equipment: none

This game is based on *'Sausage Roll'*, requiring your child to roll as they glide away from the poolside. Have your child push away from the poolside into a stretched-out, streamlined position. They roll continuously over and over, pretending they are corkscrews drilling their way through the water as they maintain their streamlined body position. Count how many times they can roll completely without losing their long, stretched-out position.

Key phrases: *'start with a big deep breath' 'keep your hands and feet together' 'stay stretched out and long'*

Progression: Add an undulating dolphin kick as they roll to increase the distance travelled.

Front Paddle

Ultimately you are teaching your child how to swim a strong and confident front paddle, sometimes called 'doggie paddle', which requires alternating and continuous arm pulls and leg kicks.

The front paddle is an *alternating stroke*, swimming in a horizontal prone (on the belly) position. Children can swim with their chin on the surface of the water or their faces submerged. The leg kick is an alternating, continuous action originating from the hips. The legs remain together as they kick, and the toes are pointed, with heels breaking the surface of the water. The arms pull in an alternating action below the surface of the water, stretching forward and pulling back with wrists firm and fingers together. Arm pulls will initially be short, and pupils should be encouraged to 'reach and pull' as they develop arm strength and confidence.

Kicking

Kicking Technique

The alternating leg kick for front paddle should be relaxed and continuous. The kick should originate from the hips so the whole leg performs the kick, and the legs move up and down with a slight bend in the knees and relaxed ankle joints. Legs should remain together with toes pointed throughout the kicking action.

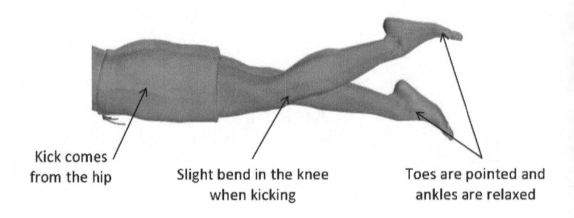

Kick comes from the hip

Slight bend in the knee when kicking

Toes are pointed and ankles are relaxed

Encourage your child to *'kick with floppy feet'* so that their ankles remain relaxed and their feet kick with a flipper-like action. Propulsion comes from the downbeat of the kick, so teach your child to kick downwards using *'the laces on their shoes'*.

39. Boil The Water

Skill: Kicking

Aim: to learn an alternating kicking action and gain confidence in water being splashed.

Difficulty: ★

Equipment: none

Have your child sit on the poolside (or steps if the pool is not deck-level) with their legs stretched out straight in front, and their toes pointed. Pretend you are in the kitchen and need to boil some water. As you turn an imaginary dial, your child begins to kick their legs as the water starts to boil. As you turn the dial in one direction or another, they increase and decrease the amount the water is boiling.

Key phrases: *'keep your toes pointed', 'kick with floppy feet'*

Progression: change the speed of the kicks by turning the heat up and down. This will develop your child's kicking stamina.

40. Volcano Eruptions

Skill: Kicking

Aim: to learn a simultaneous dolphin kick action and gain confidence in water being splashed.

Difficulty: ★

Equipment: none

Have your child sit on the poolside (or steps if the pool is not deck-level) with their lower legs under the water. Stand with your back to your child and pretend that you are a newsreader reporting on a volcano eruption. You say, *'we go live to the volcano to see if it is erupting'.* As you turn around, that is their cue to make the volcano erupt. They kick the water upwards using both legs simultaneously and continuously up and down from the knees. The more power they kick with during the upward kick, the bigger the volcano eruption!

Key phrases: *'keep your legs and feet together' 'kick upwards with power'*

Progression: see if they can kick hard and fast enough so that the water splashes over themselves.

41. Make It Rain

Skill: Kicking

Aim: to learn an alternating kicking action whilst laying on their front.

Difficulty: ★

Equipment: none

Have your child lay on their tummy and hold onto the poolside or side rail with their arms stretched straight. Use buoyancy aids if you need to. Begin roleplaying a scenario where you wonder if it will rain today. You pretend to go outside, and as you do, have your child begin to kick their legs. The faster and harder they kick, the more it will rain.

Key phrases: *'kick with floppy feet' 'keep your toes pointed'*

Progression: have you child blow bubbles or submerge their face as they are kicking.

42. Ferry Boats

Skill: kicking

Aim: to develop an alternating leg kick action whilst moving along.

Difficulty: ★ ★

Equipment: 2 floats or kickboards and floating toys

Have your child hold a float or kickboard under each arm with their forearms resting on each float and fingers gripping over the ends. Place some floating objects in the pool and have them travel to collect them. The idea of the game is to pretend that the floats are ferries collecting cargo or passengers (the floating objects) and returning them to the poolside. While focusing on collecting floaters, they are developing an effective alternating leg kick.

Key phrases: *'kick with floppy feet' 'stretch your legs out and make them long' 'make a splash behind you'*

Progression: have your child blow bubbles or submerge their face as they kick their legs and move through the water.

43. Speed Boats

Skill: kicking

Aim: to develop an alternating leg kick whilst holding one float in front.

Difficulty: ★ ★

Equipment: a single float or kickboard

Have your child hold one float out in front of them, with arms stretched out and hands holding the sides of the float. They kick their legs behind them, keeping a continuous and alternative kicking action. The float is their speed boat, and the splash they make with their toes is the engine at the back. To make the game more interesting, you could set a course they must navigate around or have them swim a certain distance against the clock.

Key phrases: *'kick with floppy feet' 'stretch your legs out and make them long' 'make a splash behind you'*

Progression: have your child blow bubbles or submerge their face as they kick their legs and move through the water.

44. *Traffic Lights*

Skill: kicking

Aim: to develop leg kick strength and stamina

Difficulty: ★ ★ ★

Equipment: a single float or kickboard

This game is a progression from *'speed boats'* where your child is kicking whilst holding a float in both hands out in front of them. You call out the traffic light colours and they respond by kicking at different speeds. When you call *'red!'*, they kick slowly. You call *'green!'* they kick fast and *'yellow!'* they kick a medium speed.

Key phrases: *'kick with floppy feet' 'don't stop kicking'*

Progression: have them kicking at faster speeds for longer to develop their leg kick strength and stamina.

45. Mermaids

Skill: kicking

Aim: to develop a simultaneous leg kick action in a supine (face up) position.

Difficulty: ★ ★ ★

Equipment: floats or kickboards

Have your child lay on their back, face up, holding a float under each arm and kick their legs, both at the same time. They pretend to be swimming like a mermaid as they kick their legs up and down simultaneously in a large flipper-like action. Encourage your child to bend their knees and kick upwards with force and power.

Key phrases: *'big kicks with your tail fin' 'kick with both legs at the same time' 'big kicks upwards'*

Progression: perform the same mermaid-like kick on the front face down with arms by their sides.

46. Space Rocket Launch And Blast

Skill: gliding and kicking

Aim: to add an effective leg kick to a glide and maintain a streamlined body position.

Difficulty: ★ ★ ★

Equipment: none

This game is very much like *'Torpedo'*, which teaches gliding. From the same starting position, you count down *'5, 4, 3, 2, 1...blast off!'* your child pushes away from the poolside as hard as possible and begins to glide across the surface of the water. After the initial push, they add an alternating leg kick, which they pretend is their rocket booster and see how far they can travel.

Key phrases: *'kick with floppy feet' 'stretch your legs out and make them long' 'make a fast splash behind you'*

Progression: have your child blow bubbles or submerge their face as they kick their legs and move through the water.

Pulling

Pulling Technique

The arm pull technique for front paddle is a continuous, alternating action with fingers closed together. The movement almost always occurs under the surface of the water, unlike front crawl or freestyle arm technique.

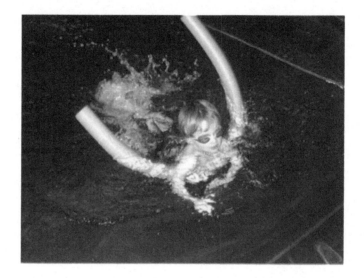

Encourage your child to *'reach and pull'* to teach them to stretch their arms forward and pull back with each arm pull. Their fingers should be closed together and wrists firm to help form a 'cup' or 'scoop' shape that they can use to pull the water towards them, generating propulsion.

47. Paddle Boating

Skill: pulling

Aim: to learn and develop a basic arm-pulling movement.

Difficulty: ★

Equipment: none

Play this game in a depth of water that your child can stand. Around waist or chest height is ideal. Have them walk through the water whilst performing a basic arm pull movement, reaching forward with their arms and pulling them back through the water, mimicking the actions of paddles on a paddle boat. They can use an alternating arm action or pull with both arms simultaneously.

Key phrases: *'reach and pull' 'make an upside down cup shape with your hands' 'keep your fingers together'*

Progression: have your child lean forward, place their chin on the water surface and blow bubbles as they reach and pull.

48. Scooping Ice Cream

Skill: pulling the water

Aim: to learn how to use the hands to pull through the water.

Difficulty: ★ ★

Equipment: none

To play this game, your child must be lying on their front in the water. You can use buoyancy aids or hold them lightly around their waist. Explain that they are an *ice cream-making machine* and that they can only move if they scoop ice cream with their hands.

Children should be encouraged to scoop using a cupped hand shape, with fingers closed together. The scooping motion should be downwards and inwards, towards themselves. As they begin scooping, move them around the pool, holding them at the surface.

Key phrases: *'make an ice cream scoop with your hand'*, *'keep your fingers together'*, *'scoop the ice cream towards you'.*

Progression: have them keep their chin on the surface of the water and blow bubbles as they scoop.

49. Collecting Candy and Treats

Skill: pulling through the water

Aim: to learn an extended arm pull action

Difficulty: ★ ★

Equipment: floats or kickboards

To play this game, your child must be lying on their front in the water. You can use buoyancy aids or hold them lightly around their waist. Explain that they will move through the water, collecting candy and treats as they do. Children should be encouraged to use an alternating arm action, extending each arm out in front before pulling back through the water. As they reach out and pull back, they collect treats and candy as they do so. Keep count, and see how much they can collect.

If you feel their arm pulls lack strength or movement, you could get your child to collect candy and *'put it in your pocket'*. This visual will encourage your child's arms to pull deeper under the water and further back, extending the overall length of the pull.

Key phrases: *'reach and pull' 'make an upside down cup shape with your hands' 'keep your fingers together'*

Progression: have your child blow bubbles or submerge their face as they reach and pull with their arms.

50. Canoe Down The River

Skill: pulling

Aim: to learn and develop an effective arm pull action.

Difficulty: ★ ★ ★

Equipment: a single float or kickboard.

Have your child hold a float under one outstretched arm, with their fingers gripping over the end. They kick their legs while pulling through the water with their free arm. They pretend they are a canoe and their arm is the ore rowing to one side. You can add to the game by chanting '1..2..1..2..' as they row down the river to help give them some rhythm. You could also add to the excitement by shouting 'crocodile!' at which point they must pull harder and faster to get to the river bank.

Ensure that your child swaps arms with the float so that both arms can practice the arm pull action.

Key phrases: 'reach and pull' 'make an upside down cup shape with your hands' 'keep your fingers together'

Progression: have your child take deep breaths and submerge their face to keep a look out for crocodiles under the water.

51. Traffic Lights - Repeat

Skill: pulling

Aim: to develop arm pull strength and stamina

Difficulty: ★ ★ ★

Equipment: floats or kickboards

This is a repeat of the 'Traffic Lights' game from the kicking section, only this time the focus is on your child's arm pulls. Buoyancy aids can be used as necessary with a woggle being the most recommended as it gives the freedom to use both arms in an alternating pulling action. You call out the traffic light colours and they respond by pulling at different speeds. When you call *'red!'*, they pull slowly. You call *'green!'* they pull fast and *'yellow!'* they pull at a medium speed.

Key phrases: *'reach and pull' 'reach far, pull hard' 'keep your fingers closed together'*

Progression: have them pulling at faster speeds for longer to develop their arm pull strength and stamina.

52. Escape The Shark

Skill: pulling and kicking

Aim: to develop alternating arm pull and leg kick actions.

Difficulty: ★ ★ ★

Equipment: woggle

Have your child push away from the pool wall with a woggle under their arms. They begin to swim using an alternating arm pull action and an alternating leg kick. After giving them a head start, you call out *'Shark!'* and begin to chase after them. This will encourage them to pull harder and kick faster as they attempt to escape the chasing shark. They win if they reach the safety of the poolside or a predetermined location within the water, such as a floating object. If you 'eat' them, they must return to the start.

The faster arm and leg actions will help to develop your child's strength and stamina.

Key phrases: *'reach and pull' 'reach far and pull hard' 'kick with floppy feet' 'pull hard and kick fast'*

Progression: encourage your child to submerge their face as they swim. Every time they do so, the shark has to stop and wait for a count of 5 seconds.

Games To Play With A Friend

121

Games to play with a friend

Playing games with a friend has many advantages. Firstly and most obviously, it is more fun. Then there is the competitive element. There is nothing wrong with healthy competition and having your child try to be better than their friend; it can only be a good thing when learning basic swimming skills.

Then there is peer pressure. This can be especially useful if your child is nervous about being in the water or trying out a specific game or skill. Having a friend, especially one that is happier or more confident in the water, can be a great source of encouragement to your child. Seeing them having fun in the water will almost certainly spur them to try it.

Safety Note:

Many games and activities in this book involve your children playing simultaneously and close to each other. Be mindful of their space because they will be too caught up in the excitement of the game to be aware. There will be a danger of collisions and bumped heads.

53. Grab A Prize

Skill: moving around and getting used to the water

Aim: to increase confidence in moving around the pool whilst competing with a friend.

Difficulty: ★

Equipment: a selection of floating toys

This game is played in shallow water and begins with randomly arranging a small selection of floating toys across the surface of the water. With your players placed approximately central to the objects, you name one, and they have to travel to it, grab it and hold it up. The winner is the first to hold the object up.

Key phrases: *'use long strides' 'use your arms to go faster' 'reach for it'*

Progression: have the players travel further distances to collect the objects, which may encourage them to swim instead of walk.

54. Simon Says

Skill: moving around the pool, floating, submerging

Aim: to enhance confidence by using a variety of skills.

Difficulty: as difficult as you want to make it

Equipment: as needed depending on the chosen activities.

You take the role of 'Simon' and issue instructions to the other players, which should be followed only when the phrase begins with 'Simon says'. Instructions can include skills such as blowing bubbles at the surface, sinking, and floating in a specific shape, depending on the ability and confidence level of the children playing the game. Each player begins with a set number of points, for example, 10 and loses a point each time they follow an instruction that does *not* start with the phrase 'Simon says'.

Key phrases: phrases that match the actions and movements that you select from previous activities.

Progression: string together combinations of skill, for example, *'star float and blow bubbles'*

55. Flip Over

Skill: moving around the water

Aim: to get used to the water and increase confidence in moving around

Difficulty: ★

Equipment: egg flips

This game uses egg flips of 2 specific colours and is played for a preset time, for example, 1 minute. Place the egg flips randomly across the surface of the water with different colours facing upwards. Before the game begins, allocate a colour to each player. On the command to start, the players move around, flipping the eggs to their assigned colour. Players can re-flip any eggs to their allocated colour that their opponent has previously flipped. The more egg flips you use, the more fun the game becomes. The winner is the one with the most of their colour after a preset time.

Key phrases: *'use long strides' 'use your arms to go faster' 'reach for it'*

Progression: have the players blow the egg flips over the change their colour instead of using their hands.

56. Sunken Treasure

Skill: submerging

Aim: to gain confidence in submerging under the water.

Difficulty: ★ ★

Equipment: a selection of sinkers

This game can be played in any depth of water. Be sure to play it in water depth that will challenge your children. Place a selection of sinkers on the pool floor, and on the command to start, the players have a set time to collect as many objects as possible, one at a time. Alternatively, you can play the game with an odd number of sinkers, and the players collect them one at a time as quickly as possible instead of in a preset time. The winner is the player with the most sinkers collected.

Key phrases: *'take a deep breath, hold it all in' 'reach down and see what you can find'*

Progression: players collect multiple sinkers in one dive to encourage them to hold their breath longer.

57. Shopping Trolly Grab

Skill: moving around the pool

Aim: to gain confidence in moving around in the water.

Difficulty: ★

Equipment: float or kickboards, floating toys

Your children will need a float or kickboard each to play this game. These will become shopping trollies. Scatter a range of floating toys around the pool. On the command to *'go!'*, each child pushes their shopping trolly (float) around the pool, collecting as many objects as possible, placing them carefully on their float, and taking them to the poolside. The winner is the player with the most on their float (in their shopping trolly). You can play this against the clock to add an element of urgency and speed to the game.

Key phrases: *'use long strides' 'use your arms to go faster' 'reach for it'*

Progression: use a mixture of floaters and sinkers so children can submerge in addition to moving around the pool.

58. Pass And Catch

Skill: moving around and getting used to the water

Aim: to get used to the water and to being splashed.

Difficulty: ★

Equipment: ball or similar object to throw and catch

Play this game in a depth of water that is not too easy but challenging for your children. Get them to stand far enough apart so they can throw and catch a ball or similar soft object. The idea of the game is to throw and catch the ball or object as many times in a row without dropping it. If a player drops a catch, the count begins again.

Key phrases: *'use long strides' 'feel the water supporting you' 'reach for it'*

Progression: use an object that sinks, and each player submerges to catch it before it reaches the pool floor.

59. Rock The Boat

Skill: submerging and breathing

Aim: to use a breathing technique whilst submerging.

Difficulty: ★ ★ ★

Equipment: none

Children play this game in pairs and begin facing each other, holding hands with shoulders under the surface of the water. One child takes a deep breath and submerges, and as they sink, they exhale using a trickle breathing technique. As they resurface, the other child takes a deep breath and begins to submerge, using a trickle breathing technique. The game continues with each child submerging and resurfacing, holding hands throughout, in a rhythmical rocking motion.

Key phrases: *'take in a huge deep breath' 'breathe out slowly' 'keep your lips tight' 'make your breath last as long as you can'*

Progression: reduce the rocking speed to slow motion, causing the breathing technique to be slower and more controlled.

60. Wood Cutters

Skill: floating, gliding and reaching

Aim: to gain confidence in stretching out across the water and floating.

Difficulty: ★ ★

Equipment: none

Children begin by facing each other, standing one foot in front of the other. With shoulders under the surface of the water, each child reaches out through the water to hold hands with the other. As their hands meet, they take hold and move forwards and backwards in a fully stretched position like a woodcutter.

Key phrases: *'stretch out' 'make your body as long as you can' "feel the water supporting you'*

Progression: perform the same activity with faces in the water, breathing out using a trickle breathing technique.

61. Tug Boat Tow

Skill: floating and gliding

Aim: to use the support of a partner to gain confidence in floating and gliding.

Difficulty: ★ ★

Equipment: none

This fun game is played in pairs and involves one child behind the other, holding the shoulders or hips, depending on the water depth of the child in front. The child in front then tows the child behind around the pool like a tug boat towing a ship. Encouraging the child being towed to adopt a flat and stretched body position is essential.

Key phrases: *'stretch out' 'make your body as long as you can' "feel the water supporting you'*

Progression: the child being towed has their face down in the water whilst blowing bubbles. Have one child lay on their back and be pulled by the other child by them, holding under their shoulders.

'People rarely succeed unless they have fun
in what they are doing.'
Dale Carnegie

Get The Best Out Your Time In The Water

Get the best out your time in the water

When spending time in the pool with your child, try to include at least one game from each of the 7 key learning skills (depending on their age and ability). The key basic swimming skills are:

- Moving around and getting used to the water
- Breathing
- Floating
- Submerging
- Gliding
- Kicking
- Pulling

For example, if your child is very young or a complete beginner, a typical 30 minute play about in the pool could include these 1-star (★) games:

- Slide And Ski (#3, moving around in the water)
- Blow It Along (#10, breathing)
- Seahorses (#18, floating)
- Take A Shower (#26, submerging)
- Sail The Raft (#32, gliding)
- Make It Rain (#41, kicking)
- Paddle Boating (#47, pulling)

For a child with a little more confidence, your time in the pool might include these 2-star (★ ★) games:

- Fetch (#6, moving around in the water)
- Slow Puncture (#11, breathing)
- Floating Stars (#21, floating)
- Lucky Dip (#29, submerging)
- Rocket Launch (#35, gliding)
- Speed Boats (#43, kicking)
- Collecting Candy (#49, pulling)

There are also the 3-star (★ ★ ★) games for those children whose confidence has grown significantly and who have made good progress.

Of course, no child will progress at the same rate for all basic skills. They may be excellent at breathing, so any 2 or 3-star breathing games will be appropriate. But, they may lack confidence in submerging, so the 1-star submerging games will be more suitable.

Don't be pushy!

Nobody likes a pushy parent, least of all a child. Children learn at their own pace, so if your child is not progressing at a particular skill, under no circumstances should you force it. Be patient. Be supportive. Be encouraging. Be nurturing. Be all those things every parent should be. If you try to force a skill or game, it will almost certainly backfire, and you will have an unhappy and reluctant child on your hands.

The Golden Rule: make it fun! No matter what. Fun is the magic ingredient to any successful learning.

How do you know when your child is safe and confident in the water?

You've spent quality time in the water with your child and had great fun teaching them to swim. If you have worked through the games in this book and had even a small degree of success, your child has gotten used to the water and is a little more confident than before you started. Well done!

How do you know when they are safe, though? If they are reluctant to play many of the games or hesitate when performing some basic swimming skills, then there is still progress to come. Every child learns at their own pace. Be patient and keep going. If it is fun, they will get there when they are ready.

If your child loves the water and is full of confidence, it could be time to test them out and see just how safe they are. A key skill that tests a child's swimming strength is their ability to change direction in the water and return to the poolside.

Have your child jump into deep water (you may want to be close by, in the water, just in case they struggle), allow themselves to become submerged and then resurface. Then have them swim away from the poolside for a distance (5 to 10 metres should be enough) and then turn around and swim back to the poolside where they started. This takes considerable strength and stamina. If they can perform this without hesitation and undue stress, then you have produced a happy and confident swimmer.

Let's not get complacent though

Just because your child can jump into deep water, swim away from the side and swim back again, does not mean that they are totally safe. **Children need supervising in the water at all times, regardless of their swimming ability.**

You've taught your child to swim. What now?

Hopefully, your happy little confident swimmer can swim a strong front paddle, sometimes known as 'doggie paddle', for a short distance without any undue stress. They may even have ventured onto their back and can happily kick themselves along whilst looking up at the stars. As a parent, your work here is done.

Taking their swimming to the next level requires them to learn a specific swimming stroke, such as front crawl or breaststroke, which means learning some swimming technique.

Now is the perfect time to hand them over to a qualified swimming instructor for structured swimming lessons. You have done the groundwork for them, and your child can now engage in formal swimming lessons that teach them specific stroke techniques.

Do you see yourself as a swimming teacher?

By teaching your child the basics of swimming, you have given them one of the most important life skills.

Have you thought about becoming a swim teacher? Giving children and adults one of the most important life skills is incredible.

I have been teaching swimming for over 30 years. I can honestly say that having the power to change people's lives is a motivating reason to go to work! Having a job for life that pays well is a huge bonus, and good swimming teachers are in very high demand.

Consider this story for a moment.

Little Jonny has just swum his first few strokes unaided. His face is filled with a mixture of surprise and pride, surprise at what has just happened and pride brought on by the praise you have heaped onto him. That pride and praise are equalled by his mother, looking on from the poolside with tears in her eyes, beside herself with joy at witnessing her son taking his first steps to master one of the most important life skills he will require for personal survival.

Who is responsible for creating this picture of achievement, pride and joy? You, the swimming teacher.

You met Little Jonny a couple of months ago when he arrived on the poolside frightened, nervous and crying, clinging to his mother's leg with no desire to go near the water whatsoever.

After gently coaxing him into the water, he clung onto you, scared as he ventured into the unknown. You then spent the next few weeks installing trust in you and confidence in himself as he built up the strength and stamina to make his way through the water.

Now for Little Jonny, his swimming lesson is the highlight of his week as he walks with great speed and enthusiasm along the poolside to meet YOU, his friend, his teacher and the person who has taught him how much fun swimming can be.

Is being a swim teacher really like this?

Yes, it is. When it comes to teaching swimming lessons, every child and adult you meet that wants or needs to learn to swim is different. Some come with no fear and have confidence built in; others are terrified and may even have a genuine fear of the water.

You can nurture and teach anyone to swim with the right skills and personal qualities you have learnt from a recognised swimming teacher's course and reading the right books. Helping people to learn one of the most important life skills whilst having fun at the same time is a very satisfying and proud feeling, and the bonus is that you get paid to do it!

Bibliography

Aqua Tots (2008) *Swimming School* [online] Available at: https://www.aquatots.com.au/news/article/?id=submerging-your-baby-the-correct-way [Accessed 18 March 2023]

Freedman, F (2009) *Teaching your baby to swim.* London, Uk: Hermes House

Mary Poppins (1964) Stevenson, R. [Film]. Burbank, CA: Walt Disney Studios.

Noble, J and Cregeen, A (2009) *Swimming games and activities for parents and teachers.* London, Uk: Bloomsbury Publishing Plc

Pixabay (2019). *Pixabay.* [online] Pixabay.com. Available at: https://pixabay.com. [Accessed 14 Feb. 2023].

Swim Teach. (2008). *Swimming Strokes | Outstanding Teaching & Learning Resources.* [online] Available at: https://www.swim-teach.com [Accessed 14 Feb. 2023].

Unsplash (2019). *Beautiful Free Images & Pictures | Unsplash.* [online] Unsplash.com. Available at: https://unsplash.com. [Accessed 14 Feb. 2023].

Young, M. (2011). *How to be a swimming teacher : the definitive guide to becoming a successful swimming teacher.* Hertfordshire, Uk: Educate & Learn Publishing.

Shutterstock images:
https://www.shutterstock.com/image-photo/grandfather-grandson-playing-together-pool-outdoor-4355356
https://www.shutterstock.com/image-photo/happy-children-wetsuits-goggles-learn-swim-1114843106
https://www.shutterstock.com/image-photo/mother-teaches-child-daughter-swim-pool-604501544
https://www.shutterstock.com/image-photo/young-mother-teach-her-little-son-713628292
https://www.shutterstock.com/image-photo/little-girl-swims-underwater-picking-toys-697353385
https://www.shutterstock.com/image-photo/mother-teaching-her-daughter-how-swim-150317858
https://www.shutterstock.com/image-photo/happy-young-father-teaching-his-adorable-1854515335

Play quotes
https://www.vincegowmon.com/playful-quotes-for-the-child-in-your-heart/
https://premiumjoy.com/blog/quotes-on-play-importance-for-kids/
https://hes-extraordinary.com/quotes-about-play
https://www.yourtherapysource.com/blog1/2019/06/06/play-quotes/

Index of Games

Games to play with a friend

An electronic version of this book is available from www.swim-teach.com

You May Also Like

How To Be A Swimming Teacher.

The definitive guide to teaching outstanding swimming lessons.

Available as an ebook to download from Swim-Teach.com or in print from most online retailers.

How To Be A
Swimming Teacher

The Definitive Guide To Teaching Outstanding Swimming Lessons

Mark Young

"Now that you have finished my book, would you please consider writing a review? Reviews are the best way readers discover great new books. I would truly appreciate it."

Mark Young

For more information about teaching swimming, learning to swim and improving swimming technique visit **Swim Teach**.

www.swim-teach.com

Made in the USA
Las Vegas, NV
04 October 2023

78550489R00083